Getting To Know...

Nature's Children

RACCOONS

Laima Dingwall

PUBLISHER	Joseph R. DeVarennes
PUBLICATION DIRECTOR	Kenneth H. Pearson
MANAGING EDITOR	Valerie Wyatt
SERIES ADVISOR	Merebeth Switzer
SERIES CONSULTANT	Michael Singleton
CONSULTANTS	Ross James
	Kay McKeever
	Dr. Audrey N. Tomera
ADVISORS	Roger Aubin
	Robert Furlonger
	Gaston Lavoie
EDITORIAL SUPERVISOR	Jocelyn Smyth
PRODUCTION MANAGER	Don Markle
PRODUCTION ASSISTANTS	Penelope Moir
	Steve Soloman

EDITORS

Mary Frances Coady   Sarah Reid
Katherine Farris   Cathy Ripley
Cristel Kleitsch   Eleanor Tourtel
Elizabeth MacLeod   Kathy Vanderlinden
Anne Minguet-Patocka   Karin Velcheff

PHOTO EDITORS	Laurel Haslett
	Pamela Martin
DESIGN	Annette Tatchell
CARTOGRAPHER	Jane Davie
PUBLICATION ADMINISTRATION	Kathy Kishimoto
	Monique Lemonnier

ARTISTS

Marianne Collins   Greg Ruhl
Pat Ivy   Mary Theberge

This series is approved and recommended by the Federation of Ontario Naturalists.

Canadian Cataloguing in Publication Data

Dingwall, Laima..
  Raccoons

(Getting to know—nature's children)
Includes index.
ISBN 0-7172-1898-8

1. Raccoons—Juvenile literature. I. Title
II. Series.

QL737.C26D56 1984   j599.74′443   C84-099569-5

Have you ever wondered . . .

where raccoons live?   page 9

where raccoons sleep?   page 10

how big raccoons are?   page 14

whether raccoons really have a black mask?   page 17

how many rings are on a raccoon's tail?   page 17

how raccoons keep warm in the winter?   page 17

when raccoons go to sleep?   page 18

how raccoons can see in the dark?   page 18

how a raccoon climbs down a tree?   page 24

whether raccoons can swim?   page 24

what raccoons like to eat?   page 27

why raccoons play with their food?   page 28

whether raccoons really wash their food?   page 28

where raccoons spend the winter?   page 32

why you might see a raccoon in the wintertime?   page 32

how many babies a mother raccoon has?   page 35

whether baby raccoons have a black mask?   page 37

how young raccoons keep warm?   page 38

how a mother raccoon protects her babies?   page 38

when little raccoons start going outside?   page 41

how young raccoons play?   page 43

when young raccoons leave home?   page 46

What do you call a bundle of fur wearing a bandit's mask?

If you answer "raccoon", you are right. And if you could spy on a raccoon as it goes on its nightly food raids, you would see that it really is, in a way, a bandit.

The raccoon's mask and its pointy face give it a mischievous look—and, in fact, most people know it best for the mischief it gets into. But there is much more to the raccoon than this. It is playful, intelligent, brave and bold.

Maybe that is why few of us manage to get *very* cross with a raccoon even if it:

—eats all the corn in our garden;

—dumps our garbage can no matter how craftily we tie the lid down;

—pounds on our door if it likes the smell of our supper;

—rolls up all the sod we have carefully laid down in the back yard; rolls it up again every time we put it back seemingly just for the fun of it.

Shall we take a closer look at this clever, spunky animal that manages to annoy and charm us at the same time?

Cousins Near and Far

The raccoon has two North American relatives: the ringtail, named for its big bushy black-banded tail; and the coati, which has such a long tail that people often mistake it for a monkey.

And did you know that the raccoon seems to have a relative living in China? Believe it or not, many scientists now believe that the Giant Panda is a member of the raccoon family!

"I'll be your friend, if you'll be mine."

Raccoon Country

Raccoons live right across North America, except in the northern part of Canada and in the mountains of the West. They prefer to live near water, usually in brushland and among trees that shed their leaves. But you will also find them in open country and farmland where there are few trees.

Raccoons have even moved into suburbs, towns and busy cities. There, they live in ravines, garages, sheds and drain pipes. Sometimes they even make their home in attics.

The shaded area on this map shows where raccoons live in North America.

A Choice of Homes

The size of a raccoon's territory depends on the amount of food in the area. If there is a lot of food available, the territory will be quite small. If there is not much food, the territory will be larger. Usually the area that the raccoon calls home covers about 2.5 square kilometres (one square mile).

Within this territory, the raccoon makes a den and lines it with leaves or wood chips. Sometimes a raccoon will even have several dens spread around its territory. You might find a raccoon den in a cave, in a hollow of a tree, or in a hollow log or stump. A raccoon may even take over an abandoned ground burrow that has been dug up by a fox or skunk.

Raccoons do not always bother going back to their den to sleep, however. Since they are active mainly at night, they have to do their sleeping during the day. At the same time, they have a decided taste for sun-bathing. So, on hot summer days, a raccoon might simply drape itself over a pile of rocks or a branch and nap in the sun.

Opposite page:

It may look like nothing but a hollow stump to you—but it is home to a raccoon.

10

The Raccoon Up Close

If you see a raccoon from the side or the back, you might think it is a large house cat. But the adult raccoons are generally bigger than cats. The average male raccoon weighs between 7 and 9 kilograms (16-20 pounds) and stands about 30 centimetres (12 inches) at the shoulder. Female raccoons are slightly smaller.

Raccoons that live in the colder, northern parts of North America are often bigger than their southern cousins. That is because a larger body tends to stay warmer in cold weather than a smaller one. When they are storing up fat to get ready for winter, the northern raccoons may eat so much that they double their weight. One monster-sized raccoon found in the fall tipped the scales at 28 kilograms (62 pounds)—about the same as an eight-year old child!

Fat, furry and ready for winter

Bandit Face and Ringed Tail

Of course, the first thing you notice about a raccoon is its mask. This is really a wide band of black fur that runs across the raccoon's eyes and down its cheeks.

The next thing you notice is the raccoon's tail. It is about 22 to 25 centimetres (8 to 10 inches) long and very bushy. It has a black tip and between 5 and 7 black rings around it. The raccoon uses its tail for balance, holding it straight out when it runs or climbs along tree branches. And when the raccoon goes to sleep, it wraps its tail around its body like a cozy blanket.

Fur Coats

A raccoon looks its best in the fall when its winter coat grows in. A raccoon really has two coats. The inner coat of brown fur is thick, woolly and warm. An outer layer of long black and white guard hairs helps protect the raccoon from the wind. These guard hairs are very smooth and water runs off them easily. So they also help keep the raccoon dry and cozy.

Glow-In-The-Dark Eyes

The raccoon's sleeping habits are different from yours. It tends to sleep during the day and come out at night. So, unlike you, the raccoon has to be able to see well in the dark.

For this reason, the raccoon has special cells in the back of its eyes that act like mirrors. At night, they catch and reflect any light coming into the raccoon's eyes. This has the effect of adding to the light and allows the raccoon to see as clearly in the dark as in daylight.

This also has an effect that can be quite startling. If you were to shine a flashlight into a raccoon's face at night, the mirror-like cells would reflect the light back at you.

Raccoons may see well in the dark, but they are short-sighted. Day or night, they have trouble seeing objects that are far away. They are also color-blind and see everything in shades of gray —a bit like watching black and white television.

Other Senses

A raccoon has excellent hearing and a keen sense of smell. It can sniff out a mouse hidden in the grass or even an acorn buried under fallen leaves. It also has a very keen sense of touch in its "fingers" and nose.

Front paw

Twinkly Toes and Nimble Fingers

The paw prints of a raccoon look almost like the foot prints of human baby. But you could not mistake a raccoon's paws for a baby's feet. The raccoon's toes are much longer, and they have short claws at the tips.

A raccoon can use its front paws as well as you can. So, unlike most animals, a raccoon is able to unscrew jars, unhook garbage-can lids and open latches. And it is smart enough to figure out how to do so, too!

Back paw

On the Move

If you see a raccoon walking, you will probably smile. A roly-poly animal, it waddles along on its short legs with its back hunched. But a raccoon can fool you. It may walk clumsily, but it can run in a burst of speed—up to 24 kilometres (15 miles) per hour—especially if it meets an enemy. But a raccoon can keep up that speed only for a short distance. To escape an enemy, it usually heads up a tree.

A raccoon is a master tree climber. It walks and even runs along branches with ease. It rarely loses its footing, but if it does, it simply curls its nimble fingers and toes around the branch and hangs upside down. Then it climbs, paw over paw, until it reaches a fork in the branch where it is able to turn itself right side up.

A raccoon feels as secure running along a narrow branch as you do on the sidewalk.

Raccoon's paw prints

Coming down a tree is just as easy. Unlike a porcupine or a cat, which always climbs down a tree tail first, a raccoon can climb down head first. That is because it can turn its back feet sideways to get a good grip on the tree.

The raccoon is also a fine swimmer. It often wades in shallow water looking for food and even swims—dog paddle style—across a pond. But it does not seem to like staying wet. As soon at it is on dry land again, it shakes itself hard to get rid of the water on its coat.

"Come on in, the water's fine!"

Good to the last drop!

Raccoon Munchies

What do raccoons eat? Practically everything, depending on what they can find.

In spring, crayfish are a raccoon's favorite treat. It wades into a pool of water and pokes its long fingers into holes and under rocks. When it finds a crayfish, the raccoon plucks it out of the water and eats it on the spot. Raccoons also fish for frogs, tadpoles and minnows, and they will feed on any field mice, turtles, garter snakes, snails and other small animals they can catch. Raccoons that live along the sea coast catch clams and oysters.

In summer, a raccoon adds berries, nuts and seeds to its diet. In the fall, it eats a lot of acorns and insects, including grasshoppers, crickets and beetles. Often a raccoon climbs up a tree and raids the combs of honey bees. It does not worry about getting stung as its thick fur protects it.

Farmland raccoons enjoy eating corn, grapes and apples. Sometimes a raccoon will even raid a chicken house for the eggs.

Water Play

When a raccoon has a meal, it does not always begin eating right away as you might do. Very often, it handles the food for a time with its front paws, usually rubbing its palms forwards and backwards over it. And if the raccoon is near water, it often fingers its food in the water.

Because of this habit, many people think that raccoons always wash their food before eating it. That is not so. In some cases, with a frog or toad, for instance, they may be getting rid of bad-tasting substances on the skin. But most often they just seem to be satisfying their curiosity or enjoying the feel of the food in their fingers. And their fingers become even more sensitive than usual when wet. So it is not surprising that they seem to especially enjoy playing with their food in the water.

Raccoons also seem to enjoy rolling pebbles and stones in their hands. And sometimes, when they are fishing for food, they will pause a while to splash about and play in the water.

Night Feeders

When darkness comes, a raccoon usually heads straight for its favorite eating place. In the woods, that could be a spring or a pond. In the city, it might be a full garbage can. Once the raccoon has had its fill, it wanders through its territory looking for more food. If it finds some, it will visit the spot the next night, often following the same path it used the night before.

Not all raccoons feed at night. Those that live along the coast feed whenever the ocean tide is low, and that is often during the day. At that time, the water has left all kinds of tasty sea creatures lying on mud flats, in shallow pools and along the beach. A raccoon will leave its den even in the middle of the day for such an easy feast.

Raccoons in Winter

Raccoons that live in the southern parts of North America are active year round. There, the temperature stays warm even in winter and the raccoon is able to hunt for food in nearby ponds and forests. But the raccoons that live in northern areas settle down in dens—usually in the hollow of a tree—to sleep away the cold winter.

Raccoons do not truly hibernate, however, the way animals like ground squirrels and skunks do. When these animals hibernate, their body temperature drops and their breathing and heartbeat slow down. This is not so for the raccoon. It stays warm and relaxed and can easily be woken up. In fact, a raccoon often comes out of its den to bask in the sun or look for food on mild winter days. But once the weather turns cold again, the raccoon goes back into its den.

The raccoon does not store food in its den for winter munching. It eats so much in the fall that it builds up a thick layer of fat on its body and does not need much food in winter.

Opposite page:

Raccoon meets beaver. There is just no telling who you will run into on a mild winter's day.

Mating Time

Raccoons mate during the warm spells of weather between late January and early March. Raccoons in the South mate about two months earlier.

During mating season, a male raccoon wanders through its territory looking for a mate. He may travel as far as 13 kilometres (8 miles) in one night. If two males want to mate with the same female, they often fight. But the stronger raccoon does not always win the female. In the end, the female raccoon chooses the mate *she* wants and turns away all others.

When two raccoons mate, they share the same den for about two weeks. After that time, the male leaves. In northern areas the female raccoon goes back to her winter sleep until early spring.

About 9 weeks after mating, the female is ready to give birth. A female raccoon usually has four or five babies in one litter, but may have as many as seven.

Two's company.

Meet the Baby

A newborn raccoon, or kit, is about 10 centimetres (4 inches) long and weighs just 60 grams (2 ounces)—about the weight of a big cookie. The kit is covered with short gray fuzzy fur.

One of the first things you notice about a newborn kit is that it does not have a black face mask or rings around its tail. These markings usually grow in by the time the kit is 10 days old.

The newborn kit cannot hear or see. That is because its tiny round ears are sealed and its eyes are shut. They will not open until the kit is about three weeks old. Its teeth will start appearing three or four weeks later.

The world looks pretty big and scary when you are only a few weeks old.

Raccoon Mom

The female raccoon raises her family alone. Her mate plays no part in looking after the young.

As soon as her babies are born, the mother raccoon licks each one with her tongue. Then she lies on her back or side with her kits around her and nurses them. When the kits are not eating, they are sleeping. They keep warm by piling on top of one another and snoozing in a big heap. If the kit on top of the pile gets cold, it wiggles around until it is snuggled into a warmer place.

The raccoon mom stays with her kits during the day. After dark, she leaves the den to find food for herself. But she always stays within hearing distance of the kits and returns as quickly as she can.

The raccoon mom protects her kits from all danger. If there is a chance that an enemy has found the den, she will look for a safer spot either in another tree or on the ground. Moving the babies is not a problem for her. She picks baby up in her mouth, by the scruff of its neck, and carries it down the tree to the new den.

Growing Up

By the time a kit is two months old, it weighs about 2 kilograms (4 pounds). At this time it starts to take short trips out of the den.

Sometimes this happens quite by accident. A curious kit may poke its nose a bit too far out of its den and tumble to the ground. The kit is rarely hurt—but always surprised.

Usually, however, the kits first come out when they are ready to climb down the tree by themselves. Together, the new little raccoons tag after their mother in single file. Although a kit nurses until it is four months old, it starts to sample grass and berries on these outings. And if it is lucky enough, it might be able to catch a tadpole, grasshopper or even a crayfish. With all this eating, the kit grows quickly, gaining about 1 kilogram (2 pounds) each month.

"Hey, Mom! Are you sure I am really ready for this?"

Fun and Games

While growing up, kits spend a lot of time playing. They race up and down trees and through branches in games of tag. Sometimes they jump over one another in leapfrog style. Other times, they wrestle, rearing up on their hind legs, charging and grabbing one another.

If a mother raccoon thinks that playtime is becoming too rough, she scolds her babies with loud growls. If that does not work, she might cuff them behind the ears or smack their bottoms.

Playtime is important for the young raccoons. By wrestling, chasing and pouncing on one another, kits learn how to hunt for food and how to protect themselves from enemies.

As the kit gets bigger and stronger, it goes on longer outings with its mother each night. Now it does not always stay close to its mother. It may trail behind her or even wander ahead. Sometimes a kit goes out with one of its brothers or sisters, or it may even go out alone.

Such adventuring can be dangerous for a young raccoon. Enemies—even wolves—do not often attack adult raccoons because they are such courageous fighters. Kits, on the other hand, make much easier targets.

But the young raccoons are safe enough as long as their mother is nearby. She will always rush to the rescue if one of her kits is attacked. And no raccoon fights more fiercely than a mother defending her kits.

Time to Go

By fall, the kits are about the same size as their mother. Even so, they will usually stay with her, in the den, through the winter.

Come spring, however, a new litter is expected and it is time for the young raccoons to leave. They are now quite ready to look after themselves and will soon be starting families of their own.

Special Words

Burrow A hole in the ground dug by an animal to be used as a home.

Cell A unit of living matter. Plants and animals are made of cells.

Den Animal home.

Guard hairs Long coarse hairs that make up the outer layer of the raccoon's coat.

Hibernate To go into a heavy sleep for the winter.

Kit Name for the young of various animals including the raccoon.

Mate To come together to produce young.

Mating season The time of year during which animals mate.

Molars Large back teeth used for grinding.

Nursing The drinking of milk from a mother's body.

Territory Area that an animal or group of animals lives in and often defends from other animals of the same kind.

INDEX

babies 35, 37, 38, 43
  illus. 36, 39, 40, 42, 44

climbing 23, 24, 41
  illus. 22, 40

enemies 38, 46
eyesight 18, 37
  illus. 19

face 5, 17, 37
  illus. 4
fall 27, 32
feeling 20, 28
fishing 27, 28
food 27, 28, 31, 32
  illus. 26, 29, 30
fur 17
  illus. 15, 16

hearing 20, 37

kits see babies

mating 35
movement 23

paws 20, 23, 28
  illus. 20, 21
playtime 43
  illus. 42

relatives 6

size 14, 37, 41
sleeping 10, 18, 38
smelling 20
spring 46
swimming 24
  illus. 25

tail 17
  illus. 16
teeth 37
territory 9, 10
  home 10
  illus. 11,12-13

North America 9
  map 9

winter 32

Cover Photo: Bill Ivy
Photo credits: N.R. Lightfoot, pages 4, 8, 29, 30, 33, 42; Bill Ivy, pages 7, 15, 19, 21, 25, 34, 36, 39, 44-45; A. Kuhnigk (Valan Photos) page 11; Wayne Lankinen (Valan Photos) page 16; Lowry Photo, page 22; B. Morin (Network Stock Photo File) pages 26, 40.

Getting To Know...

Nature's Children

OWLS

Elin Kelsey

PUBLISHER	Joseph R. DeVarennes
PUBLICATION DIRECTOR	Kenneth H. Pearson
MANAGING EDITOR	Valerie Wyatt
SERIES ADVISOR	Merebeth Switzer
SERIES CONSULTANT	Michael Singleton
CONSULTANTS	Ross James
	Kay McKeever
	Dr. Audrey N. Tomera
ADVISORS	Roger Aubin
	Robert Furlonger
	Gaston Lavoie
EDITORIAL SUPERVISOR	Jocelyn Smyth
PRODUCTION MANAGER	Don Markle
PRODUCTION ASSISTANTS	Penelope Moir
	Steve Soloman

EDITORS

Mary Frances Coady   Sarah Reid
Katherine Farris   Cathy Ripley
Cristel Kleitsch   Eleanor Tourtel
Elizabeth MacLeod   Kathy Vanderlinden
Anne Minguet-Patocka   Karin Velcheff

PHOTO EDITORS	Laurel Haslett
	Pamela Martin
DESIGN	Annette Tatchell
CARTOGRAPHER	Jane Davie
PUBLICATION ADMINISTRATION	Kathy Kishimoto
	Monique Lemonnier

ARTISTS

Marianne Collins   Greg Ruhl
Pat Ivy   Mary Theberge

This series is approved and recommended by the Federation of Ontario Naturalists.

Canadian Cataloguing in Publication Data

Kelsey, Elin.
  Owls

(Getting to know—nature's children)
Includes index.
ISBN 0-7172-1899-6

1. Owls—Juvenile literature. I. Title
II. Series.

QL696.S8K44 1984   j598.97   C84-099570-9

Have you ever wondered . . .

if all countries have owls?	page 6
whether owls come in different sizes?	page 6
what owl feathers feel like?	page 9
what the tufts on some owls' heads are?	page 10
how an owl shows it is upset?	page 10
when owls do their hunting?	page 13
why an owl's eyes are so big?	page 13
whether an owl can move its eyes?	page 14
if owls can see in daylight?	page 14
what the rings around an owl's eyes are for?	page 17
if owls make much noise as they fly?	page 18
how owls use their toes?	page 21
what an owl likes to eat?	page 22
if owls ever have problems?	page 30
whether all owls hoot?	page 33
if owls get along with each other?	page 33
how an owl finds a mate?	page 34
where and when owls lay their eggs?	page 36
how many eggs an owl lays?	page 39
what baby owls look like?	page 40
how owls look after their babies?	page 43
how owlets learn to fly?	page 45
when young owls start life on their own?	page 45

Wise old owls probably appear in more cartoons, storybooks, songs and advertisements than any other bird in the world. They seldom have starring roles, however. Mostly they perch on the sidelines looking serious and handing out good advice.

How did owls get their reputation for being so wise? Well, their large eyes always seem to be studying things. And the rings around their eyes remind us of the big, round glasses professors are often pictured wearing. In other words, they *look* wise.

But the truth about real owls is that they are no wiser than any of our other feathered friends!

Masterminds or not, owls are amazing birds. If you would like to know more about them, come read along.

Great Gray Owl

Who's Who?

Owls are found everywhere on earth, except in polar regions. From desert to forest to Arctic tundra, there is at least one type of owl for every habitat.

No matter where they live, owls are easy birds to identify. From the tiny Elf and Saw-Whet owls to the giant Great Gray and Snowy, owls look so much alike that even a beginning bird watcher can tell when he has spotted one.

Like all birds, owls have feathers, hollow bones and young that hatch from eggs. Yet owls are different from other birds in so many ways that they belong to their own special order of birds.

Most of us think of owls as rather large birds, and indeed, many are. Some, however, are no bigger than sparrows. The wee fellow you see here is a Saw-Whet. Tiny as it is, the Elf and Pygmy owls are smaller still.

Fluffy Feathers

From the top of their legs to the edge of their beaks, owls are covered in fluffy feathers. Some owls even have a thick layer of feathers all the way down to the tips of their toes. Owl feathers can be so soft that if you were to close your eyes and feel them, you could easily mistake them for fur.

Most owls have dark gray and brown markings on their feathers. These colors blend in well with their surroundings, and an owl that is sitting still is very hard to spot. So owls that hunt at night—as most do—can rest, well hidden and undisturbed, all day long.

The fluffy-feathered Boreal Owl is named for the northern forests in which it lives (boreal—of the North).

"Ears" That "Talk"

The funny tufts that stick up on the top of some owls' heads look like ears or horns, and they are usually called one or the other. In fact, they are just special feathers—but they do serve a purpose.

When an owl is resting quietly these feathers are only slightly raised above its head. The moment something upsets the owl, up shoot the feathery tufts.

If they stand up stiffly and a little forward, the owl is sending the same message a cat sends when it hunches its back and bushes out its tail: "I am ready to fight for what is mine."

Standing up but leaning slightly outward, the tufts send a less aggressive signal: "You have no business here, but I am prepared to put up with you as long as you behave."

And sometimes an owl that feels threatened will completely flatten the tufts, as if to say: "Don't mind me, I am just a little owl trying to get along."

Opposite page: It is easy to see how the Great Horned Owl came by its name. This one's "horns" are sending out a clear message: "Come any closer and there will be trouble."

10

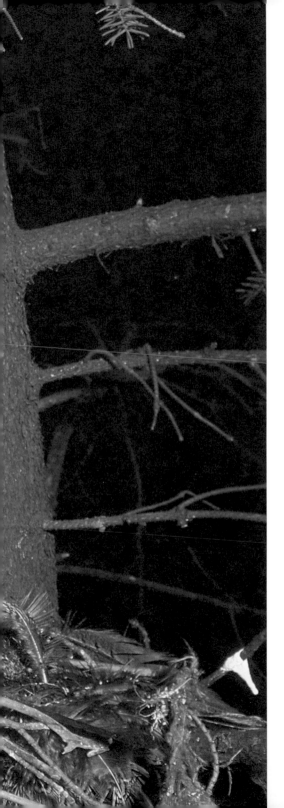

Owl Eyes

Have you ever tried to finish up a baseball game just as the last rays of evening light were fading into darkness? Remember how difficult it was to see the ball?

Dusk is the time of night when most owls start their hunting. How can they find tiny mice when it is too dark for us to see a large white baseball?

An owl's eyes are enormous. If the eyes in your head took up as much room as an owl's, each of your eyes would be the size of a GRAPEFRUIT! With such large eyes an owl can see much better in poor light than you can.

Owls' enormous eyes are especially equipped to catch the tiniest amounts of light. They are color-blind, however, and see everything in shades of gray. (Great Horned Owl and owlets)

13

But an owl cannot shift its large eyes from side to side the way you can. Its eyes are fixed in their sockets just like the headlights of a car. When an owl wants to look around it has to turn its whole head.

This is no problem for an owl, because underneath all those fluffy feathers it has a very long flexible neck. By twisting its neck, an owl can sit quite comfortably with its body pointed in one direction and its face in the other!

Many people think that owls cannot see well in daylight. Actually, they see as well in daylight as you do. But they are farsighted and do not see nearby objects clearly. In fact, day or night, an owl has trouble seeing its own feet.

Most birds close their eyes by raising their lower lid

Owls, however, lower their upper lid—just as you do.

An owl can turn its head around much farther and much more comfortably than you can turn yours—but it CANNOT turn it full circle. (Snowy Owl)

Hidden Ears

Owls could never wear earrings. Their ears do not stick out the way yours do. Instead, owls' ears are simply slits, sometimes very long, or small round holes on the sides of its head.

Even so, owls hear much better than you do. In fact, most owls hear so well that they can hunt just by listening for the tiny sounds a mouse makes as it scuttles about.

Some owls have lopsided ears—one larger and higher than the other. The sound of a mouse's movements will reach each of these ears at a slightly different time. From this difference an owl can tell exactly where the sound is coming from.

The special rings of curved feathers that surround each of the owl's eyes are called facial discs. These rings are very important to the owl because they help it hear. That's right: *hear*. The feathers in the facial discs are attached to muscles that control the shape of the ears. Just as a dog moves its ears to hear better, an owl moves these rings of feathers to locate sounds.

Opposite page: More than by anything else, we know an owl when we see one by the rings of curved feathers around its eyes. (Long-Eared Owl)

Swift and Silent

No matter how well an owl can see and hear, it would have a hard time catching anything if it sounded like a jumbo jet when it was flying.

To help muffle sounds, most owls' wings are well padded with soft, velvety feathers. The feathers along the leading edge of the wing are fringed just like the teeth on a comb. These fringed feathers also help to reduce the flapping noises that most birds make when they fly.

Try this simple experiment. Press the fingers of each hand tightly together and clap them against each other. Repeat the same thing with the fingers of both hands spread out. Much quieter, isn't it?

Like your outstretched fingers, the fringed edge of an owl's wing allows most of the air to pass right through. With their special wings, most owls can fly almost silently.

Most owls are fairly fast flyers. The Snowy, with its wing span of about 1.5 metres (5 feet), can work up to tremendous speeds, but it needs a long take-off and landing run.

Talented Toes

Apart from wiggling them, most of us do very little with our toes. Owls have many uses for their toes—perching, walking, grabbing, carrying.

All four of an owl's strong toes are equipped with hooked claws called talons. Just as you stretch your fingers out to catch a ball, owls can spread out their talons to make a successful strike.

Owls do this better than most birds because their outer toe is more movable. In fact, if they want to, they can even turn it right to the back so that it makes a pair with the back toe.

Owl's foot

This young Barred Owl has such a good grip on its perch that it is in no danger of falling off, even if it falls asleep.

Mice on the Menu

Would you eat in a restaurant that served gophers, mice and moths? You would if you were an owl. To an owl, such a menu would be DELICIOUS!

Owls never eat plants or bird seed. Meat is the only food that they can eat. The type of meat that an owl will eat depends upon how big the owl is and where it is hunting. A large owl that hunts in a meadow may eat lots of rabbits and mice. A small owl that hunts in a forest or desert may eat mice but will probably eat plenty of grasshoppers, moths and other insects as well.

Only insects and worms and the very smallest rodents have to worry about becoming a Pygmy Owl's dinner. The tiny Pygmy may weigh as little as 50 grams (2 ounces) and be no more than 13 centimetres (about 5 inches) long.

Lone Hunters

Many birds feed in large groups called flocks. To find enough food, owls need to hunt alone.

Take a minute to think of how you and your friends could collect the most eggs in an Easter egg hunt. Because the eggs are usually hidden in many different places, you would certainly find more if you spread out than if you grouped together.

Small rodents live all over the meadow and forest floor. By spreading out and hunting alone, each owl has a better chance of finding dinner.

On the watch for
a likely lunch.
(Hawk Owl)

A hunting owl will sit very still so as to surprise its prey. Perched high atop a tree, fence post or pile of rocks, an owl will wait—carefully watching and listening for rodents.

As soon as an owl has zeroed in on its meal, it swoops and pounces. The force of the pounce causes the owl's legs to bend and its talons to close.

A very hungry owl may have a picnic on the spot, but most will carry their dinner back to the safety of their perch.

Zeroed in…
(Short-Eared Owl)

A Neat Eater

Instead of picking the meat from the bones as you would when eating fried chicken, owls swallow fur, bones...everything! If the prey is small enough, they will even swallow it whole.

With owls, the work of sorting out what can be digested and what cannot goes on inside their stomach. Afterwards, the leftover bits are coughed up in a sausage-shaped pellet.

It may sound messy, but an owl pellet is actually very dry and neat. The tiny bits of bone and fur inside the pellet are just like pieces of a jigsaw puzzle. We can join enough of them back together to figure out what the owl has been eating.

Bull's-eye!
(Great Gray Owl)

Hard Times

It certainly seems that when it comes to hunting, the owl has all the advantages. But being a hunting owl is not always easy.

Like an unlucky fisherman, an owl may wait for hours without catching anything. On rainy evenings, in particular, many owls go hungry. The damp ground muffles the sounds rodents make, and it is hard for the owl to find them. Hunting is so difficult in the rain that most owls will sit out the storm and wait for better weather.

Most of the animals that owls hunt feed on plants. If a year is too cold or too dry, there will be fewer plants and therefore fewer rodents. At such times some owls will move to a new area to find food.

Barn Owls form a separate family of owls, and their heart-shaped faces and light coloring give them a quite distinctive look. Their name comes from the fact that they often nest in the dark corners of barns.

Who...Who...Who's There?

Every owl has its own section of forest or meadow that it calls home. The area is called the owl's territory.

Owls use a variety of calls to warn off unwelcome visitors. Some hoot, some whistle, and many have a call that resembles a shrill laugh. If you listen carefully on a clear night you might hear owls calling to each other. The owls in an area recognize one another by voice, and they know where their neighbors' territories are. As long as they are careful to hunt in their own backyards, the owls remain good neighbors.

This Burrowing Owl has staked out its territory on a golf course. It is not known whether the person who made the sign did so out of concern for the owl or the golfers.

Finding a Mate

In late January, a male owl's nightly calls will get louder and more frequent. This is mating season, and he is announcing his ownership of a territory in the hope of attracting females. Sometimes a female will answer with her own song, and the two will sing together in an owly duet.

Except for being a little bigger, most female owls look just like the males. Even a male owl sometimes has trouble telling the difference, and he is so protective of his territory that he may try to chase away the female he has worked so hard to attract. It often takes a lot of hooting and hollering before the male recognizes that the new bird is a female and not an unwelcome male.

To impress their new mates, male owls may perform trick flights or dance-like movements on a branch. And just as a man may send chocolates to his sweetheart, some male owls will woo their mates with gifts of tasty mice!

Some owls choose a new mate every year, but many stay together for life.

Opposite page: Unlike some owls, a male Snowy has no trouble knowing when he has attracted a female. She is easily recognizable by the dark marking on her feathers. Male Snowies are almost pure white.

Nesting Time

When it comes to nest building, owls lack talent. In fact, very few build nests at all. Instead, owls will lay their eggs in a hole in a tree, in a crack in a cliff, or in a slight hollow they scratch in the ground. Many owls will move into an abandoned nest that some other bird built the year before. There is even a Burrowing Owl that makes its home in the underground burrows of prairie dogs.

Some owls lay their eggs when the ground is still covered with snow. This may seem like a chilly time to start a family, but it means that the babies will hatch in spring—the time of year when there are lots of rodents to feed them.

Great Horned Owl

*The older owlets will soon have to move
out of the nest to give the younger ones
room to hatch and grow.
(Short-Eared Owlets)*

Happy Hatch-Day!

A female owl may lay as few as 3 eggs or as many as 12. The number depends on the type of owl and on the amount of food available. An owl that is eating well will lay more eggs than one that is not.

The mother owl lays one egg and then waits a few days before laying the next. As a result, each egg hatches at a different time. Every baby owl, or owlet, has its very own hatch-day!

The eggs need both time and warmth to hatch. So, for several weeks, the father owl will hunt for two, while mom spends all her time sitting on the eggs to keep them warm. To do this more effectively, the mother owl will probably pluck out some of her feathers to make bare patches on her underbody. That is because the feathers that keep her warm would keep her body heat from reaching the eggs.

Hungry Babies

Except for two bare strips on its back, an owlet is covered in soft white feathers called down. With its back snuggled up to mom and this fluffy down to keep in the heat, the owlet stays cozy even in the chilliest storms.

Owlets grow very quickly and have huge appetites. A week-old owlet will eat much more for its size than an adult would.

The father owl is therefore kept very busy finding food for his family. Fortunately, owls are much better at catching mice than any cat. Even so, dad may end up having to hunt both night and day to keep up with the growing appetites.

Hungry owlets make soup-slurping noises when calling for their dinner. (Snowy owlet)

Devoted Parents

By three or four weeks of age, the baby's down is being replaced by longer gray and brownish feathers. The owlets now need so much food that their mother may leave them for short periods to help their father hunt. As the owlets grow, the increasing number of dark feathers help keep them well hidden while she is away.

Owls are very protective parents. If a hungry weasel or a curious person approaches the owlets, the parents will swoop down, threatening with their sharp talons. Even the tiny owlets help to scare off intruders by hissing, snapping their beaks and puffing up their feathery coats.

Long before they are able to fly, the young owlets move into the nearby branches and plants. Often people find these owlets, and thinking that they are lost, will take them home. The parent birds know where their babies are and are taking good care of them. It is important to leave them alone.

Keeping babies fed is a full-time job for dad.
(Burrowing Owl and owlet)

Growing Up

Owls learn to fly the same way that you learned to walk or to ride a bicycle—lots of practice and lots of bumps!

As the youngsters develop their flying skills, the parents will encourage them by dangling a tasty meal from a distance. Through practice, the young owls gradually learn to hunt for themselves. By fall it is time for them to leave their parents and set up territories of their own.

The first year of an owl's life is the most dangerous. With so much still to learn about the world, many of the young owls will not survive their first winter. But those that do live to celebrate their first hatch-day have a very good chance of living to celebrate many more.

By puffing out its feathers, this young Great Horned Owl is trying to look threatening and scare away an intruder.

Owls and Us

Owls are marvellous birds and helpful too! They help farmers by catching insects and rodents that like to eat their crops. Mice would be all over everything if there were no owls.

Because most owls are active at night, it is harder to watch them as they go about their daily routine than it is to watch other birds.

As a result, there are still many things we do not know about their ways and habits. So, the next time you are out in the woods, stop, take a careful look around, and give a few hoots. Who knows, you may be the next person to discover another fascinating fact about owls.

Happy Hooting!

Special Words

Down Very soft, fluffy feathers.

Facial disc The ring of curved feathers that surround each of an owl's eyes.

Farsighted Able to see distant objects better than near ones.

Habitat The area or type of area in which an animal or plant naturally lives.

Hatch To break out of an egg.

Mating Season The time of year during which animals come together to produce young.

Order A grouping used in classifying animals and plants. An order is smaller than a *class* but larger than a *family*.

Owlet Baby owl.

Prey An animal hunted by another animal for food. A bird that hunts animals for food is often called a bird of prey.

Rodent An animal with teeth that are especially good for gnawing. Mice, rabbits, and gophers are rodents.

Talon Claw of an owl, eagle or other bird of prey.

Territory Area that an animal or group of animals lives in and often defends from other animals of the same kind.

Tundra Flat land in the Arctic where no trees grow.

INDEX

babies, 40, 43, 47
 illus. 38, 41
Barn Owl, *illus.* 31
Barred Owl, *illus.* 20
Boreal Owl, *illus.* 8
Burrowing Owl, *illus.*
 32, 42

communication, 33

ears, 10, 17
eggs, 36, 39
enemies, 43
eyes, 13, 14
 illus. 14

fall (season), 45
facial disc, 17, 47
 illus. 16
feathers, 9, 17, 18, 39,
 40, 43
markings, 9
flying, 45
 illus. 19
food, 22, 29

Great Gray Owl, *illus.*
 4, 28
Great Horned Owl,
 illus. 11, 12, 37, 44

habitat, 6
Hawk Owl, *illus.* 24
hearing, 17

horns, 10
 illus. 11
hunting, 9, 13, 25, 26, 30
 illus. 27

Long-Eared Owl, *illus.* 16

mating, 34

neck, 14
nest, 36
 illus. 37

Owlet, *See* babies

Pygmy Owl, *illus.* 23

Saw-Whet Owl, *illus.* 7
Short-Eared Owl,
 illus. 27, 38
size, 6
 illus. 23
Snowy Owl,
 illus. 15, 19, 35, 41
spring (season), 36

talons, 21, 26
 illus. 20, 21
territory, 33, 45, 47

warning
 illus. 44
Wings, 18
 illus. 19
winter (season), 34, 45

Cover Photo: Stephen J. Krasemann (Valan Photos)
Photo credits: Wayne Lankinen (Valan Photos), pages 4, 8; Michel Julien (Valan Photos), pages 7, 19, 24, 28; Lowry Photo, pages, 11, 35; Ken Carmichael (Network Stock Photo File), pages 12, 32; Stephen J. Krasemann (Valan Photos), pages 15, 37, 42; Brian Morin, page 16; Albert Kuhnigk (Valan Photos), pages 20, 38, 44; Dennis W. Schmidt (Valan Photos), page 23; Brian Milne (Valan Photos), page 27; Federation of Ontario Naturalists, page 31; J.A. Wilkinson (Valan Photos), page 41.